Through My Eyes

A LOVE STORY OF PRAYER, SACRIFICE, AND PERSEVERANCE

Ruth Allen Pryor

*b inspire*books

Published by Inspire Books
www.inspire-books.com

Print ISBN: 978-1-961065-19-2
Ebook ISBN: 978-1-961065-20-8

Printed in the United States

Contents

Chapter 1   Look through My Eyes 1

Chapter 2   God Was There All the Time 3

Chapter 3   Searching for More 5

Chapter 4   It's Working Out....................................... 11

Chapter 5   The Life of Gene and Ruth 15

Chapter 6   Love Is Not Enough.................................... 19

Chapter 7   God Will Keep His Promises 27

Chapter 8   Gene and Ruth -1972 35

Chapter 9   Working through Tough Times 43

Chapter 10 Training to Be Men 45

Chapter 11 The Angel in the House - "Baby Named Corry" .47

Chapter 12 Supernatural 53

Chapter 13 It Hurts 63

Chapter 14 God Heard My Cry 67

Prayer...71

About the Author...75

CHAPTER 1

Look through My Eyes

All that the Father giveth me shall come to me; and
him that cometh to me I will in no wise cast out.

—John 6:37

*J*was born Ruth Bell Allen on April 24, 1941, in Gaffney,
South Carolina, to a small-town father Oliver Allen,
mother Lillie Manning Allen, and I was one of thirteen
children in my family. I'm the third child with ten siblings under
me. I remember being a small little girl playing around the house
at the age of eight years old, and I started experiencing GOD
dealing with me.

I couldn't understand when I would go to church and I would
sit beside my mother in revival service and the preacher was
preaching it was like something was frightening to me. I didn't

understand what was happening to me at all—I just knew God was calling me.

I wanted to get up, but I didn't know what to say. If I would've pulled on my mother, she would say, "Stop" and "Be quiet." One thing about those times when I was coming up, you didn't talk in church when the preacher would say, "Come to Jesus—he will save you."

Something kept pulling me, but I wanted him to stop. God's Spirit was drawing me, and I didn't know what to do with that.

So that's when I realized I didn't want to go to "HELL." All I knew was that I needed to be good and to obey my father and mother. When my parents called me for anything, I was there to do whatever they asked of me because that is how I was raised.

I worked hard on the farm. We had cotton, corn, cane, to-bacco, wheat for flour, corn for cornmeal, cows for the milk, and hogs for meat. We had mules to plow the fields, and we made our own soap to wash our clothes. We made our own butter and lard to cook with and our own syrup.

We worked so hard in the field trying to get out the cotton before winter. Sometimes it got so cold we couldn't pick it; we just pulled off the bowels from the stock and carried them inside to finish packing in the warm house out of the cold so Daddy could carry it to the gin to get paid and to get seed for the next year's planting season.

"HELL IS NOT FOR ME"

When I was getting older, I thought more and more about God. I still didn't want to go to hell, and I would pray so hard every day and night. All through the day, I was afraid I was going to hell. I didn't understand, but I couldn't give up on God.

CHAPTER 2

God Was There All the Time

Pray one for another, that ye may be
healed. The effectual fervent prayer of
a righteous man availeth much.

—James 5:16

When I was about twelve years old and supposed to be
shucking corn in the barn, I was swinging and cut my
foot on a rusty nail. I was cut so deep I called, "GOD,
my GOD, heal my foot!"

It was so bad it looked like I should have seen a doctor, but to-
day it looks like it's sown up by a doctor—but it was Doctor Jesus.

Still carrying the scar, this was the first miracle and,
oh my God, this is just the beginning!

As I remember, we only had one doctor in our town in those days when we would get sick. (We had all kinds of herbs and remedies we made, and we would take what we made.)

One year later, I had another accident. I was working out in the field. I went to use the restroom in the woods. I tripped and fell on one of the stalks, and it pierced my body. I was hurt so bad and was bleeding profusely. I called on my God again, and he healed me.

Now I know he hears my prayers! This was the second miracle performed in my life.

CHAPTER 3

Searching for More

Trust in the Lord with all thine heart; and lean
not unto thine own understanding. In all thy ways
acknowledge him, and he shall direct thy paths.

— P r o v e r b s   3 : 5

*A*s I said in the previous chapter, I knew God listened to my prayers and that I must focus on God. I talked to him every day and thought of him all through the day while working in the field. I would go ahead of everybody and pull off my sack and go to the ditch; it was so deep, so no one could see me praying and crying. I knew it was more I needed from God.

Just like in the evening when we went home, I would get my work done so my father and mother didn't need me for anything else. Now it was my time, and I would walk in the woods and lay on the porch on my back and look up and dream of places I would like to go. Some days we wouldn't go to school. Where we lived, I had friends and we visited each other on Sunday. We had an old car that didn't run, and I used it for my place of prayer. I loved talking to God rain, snow, hot or cold—this was my safe haven.

I just loved talking to God, and in that I thought being good you could just go to heaven, but in the back of my mind, I knew there had to be more to it than that. I needed more. I was looking for answers. I didn't know just what that was at the time, but I couldn't stop praying and searching for more—I never gave up.

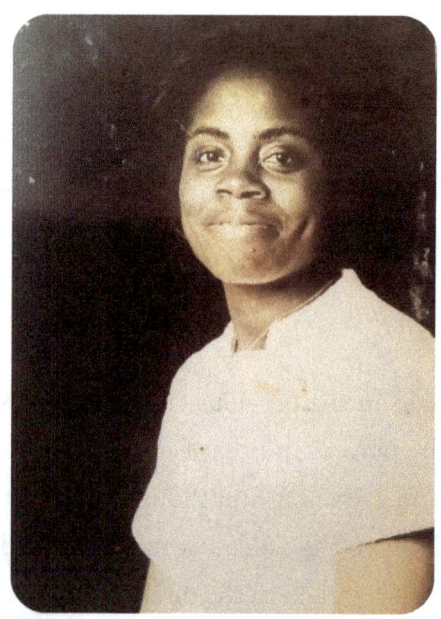

I couldn't read very well when I was small. We had a little white school that had two rooms with two teachers who taught everyone. I was five years old at that time, and I was too young to attend school, so my aunts and my cousins would carry me to school while my mother worked.

When I grew up, I found some old nonfiction books someone had thrown away, and that's how I learned to read. I would read every chance I got.

We were not able to go to school much since we had to work on the farm. God taught me how to read, and that's why I talked to God like I did. He was everything to me. I could tell him all about my pain, my hurt, and my desires that only God could fix.

As I was growing up more and more, I was able to start working away from home. Every day, I would go to pick peaches. Around this time, I was about sixteen years old, and boys started to like me.

Lord knows I was too young for boys but not too young to pray. I was afraid; I knew boys were trouble at that time. I didn't need the trouble, my Lord, because my father and mother taught us the right way, and I feared if I didn't obey God and my parents, I would have to suffer for that. I didn't need a boyfriend that had so many girls in his life. He had to have respect for me first, then my parents, and that was a must.

At the age of seventeen years old, boys started coming to see me, but they were not for me, and they were not in God's plans for me. I let my guard down and got my heart broken, and it hurt so bad. I even got engaged, but I didn't like the pain. I had to go to that old car that I would sit in to pray. I always prayed. I had to get in touch with God because God knew my heart and my desire, and I was trying to keep myself pure. I asked God for a man who would love God with all his heart, soul, and mind and who would love me and do right by me. He had to be God-sent because God knew my heart.

I started to talk more to God about my life, what I wanted in a husband, and my children. I was talking to this old man on our job who was our foreman, and he said to me, "Ruth, that is not a man; you want God. There is no man like that one. Only God can make it happen."

Then at that time, God started to work on my behalf and just know the devil started trying to put doubt in my heart. He said, "You don't go anywhere," and I had to fight that spirit. All I knew was that I know God had answered my prayers before. I said, "Lord, I don't know where he is, but send him wherever he is." I did not know who it was or who it was going to be or where he was coming from.

I later learned that when I was praying for him, he was praying for me at the same time he was in Washington, DC. The man for me had to love God. I would not ask for anything less; I dared not.

CHAPTER 4

It's Working Out

If ye shall ask anything in my name, I will do it.

—John 14:14

Whatever you want to ask for pray and believe and you can have. In 1962, I went to work in Shelby, North Carolina. I lived with my cousin and went home on the weekend. Well, I began to see God working! It was really God's plan, but I didn't know it at the time. I just kept praying and trusting God for my life. What I wanted in my life, only God could give it to me. God had plans for me and my husband and children. I asked God for my family, and he heard my prayer.

My Blessing Is on the Way

Before my dream could come true, Satan was trying to sidetrack me with temptation. It was testing time again! I found out that Satan did not stop. I tried to be good, and I didn't want to go to hell, but being good was not good enough. One day, a man came to see me. Oh God, he was married.

Girls, watch—that is a bad road to go down. Sin has hidden his face. When you get a little older, your flesh will try to control you, and I was afraid of what would happen to me.

The Bible says to watch and pray because sin will cause God not to hear you (Isaiah 59:2): "But your iniquities have separated between you and your God, and your sins have hid his face from you, that he will not hear." The devil knew I wasn't experienced, so he wanted to block the plans that God had for me. My whole life, I was on this path that God had plans for me, and I had to trust God and wait cause the devil comes to kill and destroy (John 10:10). I was brought up that if I wanted to date or see a boy, my brother had to go with me, just going to the movies or anything like that. But I trusted and waited on God because I knew I was being put to the test.

In my flesh we were fighting again, and in my spirit, I was fearing God, and with my parents, I was being tested. Only God could help me and keep me. I knew I didn't know much about life; I had not experienced the world. Praying and talking to God is what kept me.

Someone might say, "Ruth, why do you talk about God all the time?" Just keep reading. I hope when you finish this book, you will see why and you too will talk about him.

God Is Faithful

Prove all things; hold fast that which is good.
–1 Thessalonians 5:21

If ye shall ask anything in my name, I will do it.
–John: 14:14

If ye love me, keep my commandments.
–John: 14:15

I hope one day you, too, will realize there is more to life than good times, partying, drinking, drugs, sex, lots of money, women and men, all type of things. One day, you will have to look in the mirror and face yourself. What will you see—a smile or a frown?

Pick One

One day, I was at home before I met my true love. I was sad that day. I had a friend who didn't come by every week like I wanted him to. I really wanted to see him, so I prayed and asked God to send him my way, and as I got up off my couch, I saw him pass by the window and heard a knock on the door. My God, you did it again, and it was so quick!

But he was not in God's plan for me. But look, what I'm saying is God has worked miracles! If you believe in God's Word and pray with all your heart and mind, you will see it. But you haven't seen nothing yet—well, let me tell you.

CHAPTER 5

The Life of Gene and Ruth

The steps of a good man are ordered by the
Lord: and he delighteth in his way. Though
he fall, he shall not be utterly cast down: for
the Lord upholdeth him with his hand.

—Psalm 37:23–24

One day, my uncle came to me and told me that he had a cousin that wanted to meet a good girl he could settle down with. Of course, the cousin didn't know me, and I didn't know him, so my uncle told the cousin that his wife had a niece who he needed to meet.

I really didn't know much about him, and every time he tried to see me, something would go wrong and get in the way. The plan would always fall through, but we talked on the phone. It had gotten so we fell in love, and we hadn't even met yet! We didn't even know what each other looked like. Lord, I cried and prayed that this was the one who was in God's plan for me.

One day, there was a knock on the door, and I opened it, not knowing who was behind the door on the other side, and I looked and a smile came over my face as I saw who it was. And there he was—I almost fell on my face. He asked me my name first with a smile, then he asked me out. Lord, I had never been out with a boy before. He took me to a club, and I never been to one before, so you know I was out of place.

I was afraid that God would see me and would not be pleased with me. I wasn't brought up like this. I was so uncomfortable! Then he went and played a record, *These Arms of Mine* by Otis Redding. He held me so close and so carefully, like I was so fragile, and when he took me in his arms, it was like time stopped.

I had found my true love at last. I was so happy and afraid all at once. He wasn't saved yet, but I knew he was in God's plan. I had found my other half, and my life was never the same again—only God could do it.

Now the Test Is on Its Way

At this time, I was not living at home. I had a job away from home, but after a while, my job ended, and I had to move back home. There were some lonely times, nights, days, and weeks, and Lord knows I was missing him so much, but he didn't have a car yet. He had to borrow a car to come to see me, and we lived miles away from each other. Boys didn't come to see girls every week. Maybe every two weeks if he had a car or once a month if he didn't have a car. But he had my heart. I been praying ever since I was sixteen years old for my soulmate, and God had always been there for me, and I knew he would never leave me now.

Because praying had always got me through, I trusted and hoped God brought Gene in my life and that God had a special treasure just for me—that was my prayer. Satan knew what was ahead; we didn't know, but he did. I had many tests and trials to go through, I had no idea.

> *Satan don't give up; that's why you don't give up*
> *on God, and he won't give up on you.*

It had been some time now, and one Sunday evening, when I had been to church, I had on a black dress with a wide skirt on it and a wide black belt. On my shoulder, I had a white rose and had on a pair of black pumps. It had been a long day, and the day was almost over.

At eight o'clock, a truck pulled up. The lights was so bright, I couldn't see! Lord, and the porch light was even brighter.

Then my grandmother got out and went in the house, but she came back out on the porch and said, "Ruth, Gene is in the truck. It's almost eight-thirty, and you had to be on your way out," not coming in after she told me he was in the truck.

I said, "Grandmother, don't say that." I was almost in tears.

She said, "Come in, Gene."

I said, "Don't do this to me," then the truck door opened, and he came out running to me. I ran to him, and it was like my whole world had stopped. I didn't see Dad, Mom, or Grandma.

We only seen each other. With his arms open, all I know was that I was back in his arms again. I almost passed out—it was like slow motion.

When God is in the plan, it will be like this. We had to wait on the Lord and trust him that he would come through. We loved each other enough to get married then, but the time wasn't right. We still had to wait on God. We were young, we had no home, no job, or car—all we had was each other.

CHAPTER 6

Love Is Not Enough

A man's heart deviseth his way: but
the Lord directeth his steps.

—Proverbs 16:9

W e were trying to hold on, and Satan knew it—Lord, now we have a big problem. Our flesh was fighting us hard it got the best of us, and we failed the test. I felt so bad. I felt I had betrayed the Lord, and I was so sorry. But me being back home helped me. Gene and I didn't get to see each other very much; we would call on the phone. God forgave me.

We were not ready. We would only be there because the flesh and our marriage could not stand the pressure. We both kept praying for each other, not knowing God's plan. I said the Lord looked in his treasure and got someone he picked just for me. When we first met, I knew God was in this.

When you read further along in this book, you will see that God has a plan. Don't do it yourself.

Although Gene wasn't saved yet, for me, trying to be good is not being saved. The Lord said he that believe that Jesus came and took upon himself and died for our sin is saved. John 3:16 says for God so loved the world that he gave his only begotten son that whoever believes in him should not perish but have everlasting life.

It took a while before we got saved; always know your flesh can be your worst enemy. It was hard, but now I was back home. I didn't hang around with a lot of girls, just my close friends and family. We were brought up in the same church and doing church work. For my dream to come true, I had to go through something. I tried to watch myself, and I had to have respect for me. I wanted to be faithful to the man of my dreams, so I wanted to wait for when the time was right. It will happen—you can have what you want if you have respect for yourself, and he will show you respect. I wanted to carry myself so when I got married my husband would know he could trust me.

I won't say you won't fall, but don't lay there! Get up and ask God to forgive you. Don't keep doing it.

I hadn't stopped dreaming and trusting God that he had my life planned out. I just had to wait on God's time; his time is not our time. We just keep waiting on the Lord and praying. With the prayers I prayed it would come true—we just had to wait for the right time.

About two years later, Gene came to my house and asked, "Will you marry me?" I was so afraid, not of him but his lifestyle. I tried to think of something to hold him off for a while. I wanted to be his wife, and I loved him, so I said, "Well, I don't have a ring."

We were getting ready to go down a road I hadn't been on before. Life was about to take on a whole different meaning. The next two weeks, he came back with my ring. His lifestyle, I couldn't get it out of my mind, but he had my heart. So, I just came up with something like, "Buy me a car."

Well, he went back, and he stayed away for two to three weeks, then he came back and drove up in a green and white 1955 Oldsmobile and gave me the keys. He said, "Now please will you marry me?"

The next thing was, "You must ask my dad."

I really loved Gene, so he called my dad to the side and went walking. That was a tough one—I was the oldest girl at home at the time. So, Dad said yes, and I was still trying to make sure it was God. I had one more thing I had to do. I had to talk to me, myself, and I.

It was a question I had to ask myself, and this is what I said: "If I got married to another man and Gene came by, what would I do?" I would go with Gene; you see, Gene had my heart, but if I married Gene, I would never look back. The body without the heart is no good that is why God looks at the heart. So, we went and got married on Sunday March 7, 1965. Yes, we were married, but I didn't stop praying. He was not saved yet, and, on the weekend, he would go out, and I would help him get dressed to go out.

I was talking to God and crying, yes, crying—he had my heart. He liked dancing and partying. I didn't go. I stayed at home, I didn't go out with other women, I had about two young ladies that were my married friends that I might visit, and I always visited older ladies. I would help the ladies can homemade jellies and sew and just go and talk and get some advice from older mothers; I liked talking to them. In my life coming up, I always respected and talked to them. The greatest teacher I had to teach me was my mother, who taught me how to be a good and faithful wife and mother. No matter how tough life got, she held on, and I watched her.

I kept my house clean, my floors shining, and cooked, trying to take care of my duties as a wife. I would get dressed up just for him. Remember, I never gave up on prayer, sometimes crying and staying up all night looking out of the window waiting. I never told my father or my mother about what we were going through. Take your problems to God and leave them there. God sees it all, and he will fix it—he is the only one that can. My family was never brought in on our problems; our marriage problems stayed in our house.

I am trying to help someone out there learn how to treat their mate—husband how to love your wife and wife how to love your husband. Never let your marriage grow cold, never let your marriage be dull, and always keep it exciting with candlelight and soft music.

Satan knew he was trying to discourage me, but I kept praying. Gene would go out on the weekend, and he would work hard to take care of his home and his bills and me. On the weekend, it was party time, and he kept going. I had to stand still and wait on God. I knew my husband and I were in God's plan.

He wasn't saved yet, and we had been married for about two years and talking about having a family, but the time wasn't right yet. When I did get pregnant, I couldn't hold onto it. I was so stressed out, and I was not able to carry them full term. The thing I did was call on God, and he never let me down. I said, "Lord, don't let me have a child until Gene is saved," and God heard my plea.

Now, the Lord was chasing him, and Gene knew his time was running out and party time was about to be over. The world had my husband so bad; Satan knew Gene would give him so much trouble once he got saved. For three Saturday nights straight, he would go from one place to another. The first night he went, the second he went, and the third night he went and asked God to give him one more night, and he would come in. God told him, "If you don't, you will die."

The third night, he went out and picked some friends up, and they were on their way for the last good time. He was going down the road and something happened to the car. He said it was like he ran over something big in the road. The whole car shook, and he got out to see what it was, and there was no one there. Everybody wanted to know what was wrong, and he said, "I know what it is—it's time for me to go home." He never went out again, and he stopped smoking, stopped drinking, stopped clubbing, and gave up the ladies.

After that, he never went out again, and he came home to me for good. This occurred in 1967. Gene always took care of me and all our bills. I didn't have to worry about anything. Thank God he came in and never looked back. He worked hard and made sure my needs and wants were taken care of. Gene was always a good provider; he just had a hard time coming out of the world. He was running from God.

When he gave all that up, I became pregnant, and I was able to hold on to this baby. Before she was born, he was saved, and we had started going to church with our neighbor. We both sat down and talked about our lives again and asked each other for forgiveness of our past lives; we didn't need to bring our past into our future.

Also, with sins of our flesh out of control, God said it is better to marry than to burn. We didn't wait on our love we had for each other; we didn't wait, and that was sin. To begin right, we had to ask God for forgiveness so we could end up right. With everything, it is the only way we could go and trust each other; we loved each other, and this would make our lives and our marriage strong, and we would have faith in each other.

Don't forget—we were in God's plan. This you will see: If you want God in your life, trust God, pray, and read his Word. Keep calling and keep calling, and whatever you do, don't give up on God. Sometimes, what we want may not be the right time; God's time is always on time, but you must have faith in him. If you try to do it yourself, no matter what it is, it won't work without God.

CHAPTER 7

God Will Keep His Promises

Thou wilt keep him in perfect peace, whose mind
is stayed on thee: because he trusteth in thee.

—Isaiah 26:3

When we got saved, God put our marriage together, and now God had worked another miracle in our lives. I was so sick, but I kept fighting to bring my baby to full-term. Satan didn't want this to happen. (You will see why later in the book; it was a miracle, and it was God's plan). We were going to church every Sunday and getting our lives together; we were very happy.

Satan wasn't happy, and he was trying to discourage us, but our minds were made up to serve God. Gene was saved now. I had asked God to not give me a child until he was saved, and God honored my prayer. Oh yes, Satan was not giving up that part of life. When you serve God, prayer will overpower anything that the enemy can come up with.

When Gene was young, he went to school, but he didn't learn how to read. His mother died when Gene was twelve years old, and his father died when he was thirteen years old. His mother was a teacher before Gene was born, but his older brother and sister, aunt and uncle, took care of the young children, and he had to become a man early. God had plans for him, but God wanted to get the "glory"—he will and he must. Every Sunday, he would go up for prayer. God said, "I'll meet you at the altar," so he went. Every time he went to the church, people were talking about him going up there so much, they thought Gene had backslid on God, but they did not know he was fighting for his life. Gene was in God's plans, and Satan knew it.

One day, he got the Bible and was trying to read it and asked me to help him read. This caused us both to read together. We kept going; every time a church door was open, we went. We had been going for some time now, and Gene was beginning to be chased by God. One day, God called Gene and said, "I need you to preach the Word." You just don't know; we didn't see that coming.

All I could think was, "Gene, the people won't hear you." They could be so cruel sometimes and would hold your past against you. "How you were in the streets, and I was afraid."

Gene knew he wasn't prepared, so he said, "God, I can't go. I can't even read your Word." He lay down on the couch, and a miracle began to happen. It was like heaven opened up and seeds came pouring out on his head. He stopped. I can't take it anymore! It finally stopped, and he got up reading. It was a supernatural miracle—he had said to God, "I can't go," but who God calls he qualifies.

God was showing him you got work to do; he could only read the Bible. If he got distracted or stopped praying like he did, the words in the Bible would go away to a clean sheet of paper. He had to lean on God all the way. Everything he did, he went to God about it. He just kept on searching for more of God, praying and looking for answers, waiting on God. He was still trying to learn all he could about the Lord.

I was saved also. I had tried smoking, too, while we were at Walls Memorial. Everything was good, God was blessing us, but we didn't see the next move. At first, the little house we lived in, the rent was too high, and it went up to $49.00 a month. Sometimes, his bring-home pay was $27.00 a week, sometimes more or less, so we had to move from the home we rented. The church we were attending the pastor said there is a new house next door to him, and it had just been built. We went to see the man about the house, and it was in 1968. The man said move into the house, so the pipes won't burst. Look at God!

Our baby girl Betty was two weeks old. Our house payment was $69.00 a month; it was a gift from God. When she was born, it snowed three times while I was in the hospital and after we moved, a bigger snow came. Gene was not able to go to work, and we had just $1.50. The snow was so deep you couldn't drive a car. He went to the store on foot to get food. He brought a can of PET milk for the baby, one carton of milk, and a two-pound bag of corn meal for both of us, but we were still happy and thankful to God.

We didn't know how we were going to pay $69.00 a month, but he let us move in without a down payment. It was God, and he did it again; we stayed there a month or two, and God was showing us he was with us all the way. Due to the snow, Gene was not able to work for three weeks, and after one month, we were able to invite my mother, father, my sisters and their husbands, my pastor, my uncle from my hometown, the pastor next-door, and his wife. God showed up again, and we had so much food I didn't have room enough to put it all.

God said if you pay your tithes, he will open the windows of heaven and pour you out blessing you won't have room enough for them (Malachi 3:8–10). God did just what he said. My home church pastor blessed our house and prayed for Gene and I. God is so good to us; we have used our home for blessing the people of God. "Thank you, Lord."

Later, the church made Gene the treasurer while we were there. One day, we heard there was an outdoor service in a yard under a big oak tree. Gene went and came back and said, "Ruth, you need to come and hear the preacher." I didn't want to go. It was one of those holy sanctified churches, and I always was frightened the people were shouting and jumping and was just loud. At the church where we were going, they sang, shouted, and clapped their hands. I didn't know at the time that one must live holy. In

1 Peter 1:15-16 God said be ye holy for I am holy. This is God's Word. One night, I decided to go, and it was different. It scared me, and I didn't understand, but I just kept going. At first, I didn't want any part of it; I just wanted to stay away, but I couldn't. I started praying about it.

One night, Gene and I went, and a young man was preaching and when he called people up for prayer, I was trying to go up; every time I tried, he was standing on the porch. Someone always got in front of me and blocked me. I was still trying every night for two weeks of revival, so when I could go, I would. One Thursday night, I went up and was able to reach the top step and then to the porch. All at once, the Spirit that was pulling me at the age of eight years old came back to me, and I cried like a baby.

That Holy Spirit that I was so afraid of was what I needed, and I rededicated my life back to God. You see, the Lord was so good. Every time I got a chance to go to the altar, I did. The young preacher was sixteen or seventeen years old at the time, and God was using him mightily.

Gene and I were still in church next door at Walls Memorial. God brought us a long way. Gene had learned how to give hymns at the church. The deacons took him under their wings, and the sisters and mothers took me. We will always be thankful for our friends and the saints that have been in our lives; it was all in God's plans. We were there for a few years. Now God had blessed us with two children; we had our son named Charles. When God has plans for you, whatever he says, go or come, you must obey; we learn as we go. We kept seeking God, and whatever God said, we did it. As you continue reading this book, you will understand.

The Days of our Lives

Our lives were always in God's hands and his plans. At the oak tree in the community, the bishop that held the outdoor services started a church in a little white house named Follow Peace Holiness Church of God. The pastor's name was Bishop Samuel Martin. We started going to that church. Gene and I were very busy working in the church, and he was strong in the faith. Gene would not move from God's Word. God said be perfect, and some people couldn't understand. They would say you can't live perfect.

Matthew 5:48 says, "Be ye therefore perfect, even as your Father which is in heaven is perfect." Even if he didn't understand, he would never deny God's Word. No matter who said you can't, God said it, and that was enough for him. You can't live perfect before man, but you can before God. God looks at the heart, and man looks at the outer appearance.

I was now a part of the choir, so we were very busy after a few years, Gene was ready to accept the calling on his life to preach the gospel. God called him seven years before, but he was waiting on God's timing, and God had blessed us with another son David. Gene was now a Sunday school teacher, a deacon, and he also drove the bus and supported the pastor. Anything I could do to help in the house of God, he said first you must be humble enough to do the little things before you can do the big things. For many years, I had to be tough and obey God and my pastor. One day, God said to Gene, "I want you to carry my Word and go preach the gospel." God called Gene in the year 1969, but he could not read the Word yet, but God was still showing us that whatever we went through, he would be with us.

CHAPTER 8

Gene and Ruth -1972

Let us hold fast the profession of our faith without
wavering; for he is faithful that promised.

—Hebrews 10:23

Gene answered the call to preach in the year 1972, and the
first sermon he preached was called "God Hires and Fires."
I was raised to obey my pastor. As Gene accepted the call
to pastor, I realized that as my pastor he would rule over me as
a member of the church, but God would rule over him and over
the entire church.

We have always had many people stay in our home. When
our church had conferences or revival meetings, people from out
of town would come. We served many families, couples, senior
citizens, children, and young people. God blessed us, and we tried

to bless God's people. As Gene preached, we were with Bishop Martin for about eight to nine years. Then Bishop sent Gene and I to pastor a small church.

It had been a house, and it was turned into a church in Gaffney, South Carolina. We had a few members, and we had another daughter named Nicole. With the members, we had we trained our children how to give out hymns, pray, take up offering, and sing in the choir. We were teaching and trying to bring them up like the Lord told us to. The people started coming, men and women from the street, and God was truly blessing. If you could see what God was doing, some people came in that had been on drugs, alcohol, and all kinds of problems. They came on in just to hear Gene preach.

These were the kinds of people who were not accepted in big churches, which meant God was not accepted. When the evening church services were over, we would load up as many in our car that it would hold and take them home. The police came by and thanked Gene while he was preaching. Crime had gone down; it was a blessing for the city. He just wanted to say, "God bless you, sir." We could never put them out. We went to serve, not be served. God came for the sinners that they might be saved. God so loved the world that he gave his only begotten son that whoever believes in him should not perish but have everlasting life (John 3:16).

I thank God for my salvation. That's why we were trying to bring our children up right so when they get old, they would know the way and if they depart, they will know how to come back. As Gene preached, I tried to always be by his side, not in front but by his side. We were under Bishop Martin for many years, and Gene learned how to pastor, how to be a deacon, and how to be a teacher. He also learned how to see about the needs of the people. When you love God, you will help the needs of others. By this time, we had met and worshipped with a lot of great saints and met some real God-fearing saints who loved God. Gene and I knew God had been with us all our lives. We had seen miracles, signs, and wonders, and God was not through with us yet.

A New Opportunity

Gene and I had a friend who came to see us and asked Gene to come and pastor one of his churches. He had two, but some said Rev. Pryor was too young, and it was a church that had a lot of trouble.

Gene said to them, "I am a troubleshooter, and if they didn't have a problem, God wouldn't need me there." Gene said, "I will try it."

The pastor who called for him was Rev. Darvin Ross, and the church was White Oak Springs Baptist Church. Gene was there for two years, and then he said, "You can ordain me now." He had to be ordained into the Baptist church. He was already ordained under a bishop, and he needed to be ordained under a Baptist minister in a Baptist church. Gene would not move without God leading him.

We got sat at White Oak Springs, and Rev. Pryor had seven members who were older. Starting off with God's number seven. We started our children singing, and we made a small choir, and we named it the Sunshine Choir. Gene and I went out to talk to members who had left so they would come back. Some of them knew Gene when we were in the world, but they didn't know that he was a preacher.

One of the ladies said, "We will come, but you won't be able to stay."

He was not the old Gene they knew from the club; he was a new man. Old things have passed away and behold all things become new, and he was a new creature.

We had church the first and third Sundays. Gene went to God in prayer because he needed to know what to do next. God let him know to start having church every Sunday. This was a big change for them. The church had started growing, and Gene had to start everything over or just start fixing things. Yes, it was hard, but the battle belongs to God.

Yes, I had cried many times over the years. People will show you who they really are; it took prayer and fasting, and after a while, children started coming, and the parents started coming. We were praising God; they were not used to being in church lifting their hands to God. They didn't worship in church like that, so Rev. Pryor had to start from scrap with them and to let them know that God is a Holy God, and we must worship him in spirit and in truth. He had to preach that you must live holy; if not, you can't go to a holy heaven. You must be born again. The older members thought you could go to heaven by being good, and it won't work. Ask me how I know; I thought the same for years until I learned.

Rev. Pryor said, "I don't do anything without asking God first." We went to White Oak to serve, and to serve God, you must serve the people. He had to change some things, and we don't like change. God blessed, and many souls were saved at the church. God blessed beyond our wildest dreams! We grew from 7 members to about 300 members. Rev. Pryor preached near and far during that time; he went all over the country.

He even took me to the place I dreamed of when I was a young and I wanted God to let me go there someday, and my prayer was answered. The city was New Orleans. Gene preached there, and that is another prayer that came true.

God will never let you down. You may let him down, but if you just live for God, whatever you ask God for, he will give it to you. Just believe and trust him. I look back over my life, and I can see many miracles he has done in my life, some instantly and some later, but he has always answered. Try God—I hope and pray that someone reading my book will see and know that God is real.

The plans God had for Gene and Ruth, only the two of them could carry it out. We had many tests in life; people came and went, that is life. It will keep you on your knees. We prayed, we fasted, and he would go away to be alone to pray for two weeks or more. Whenever the Spirit of God led him to do it, and the bigger the problem, the longer he would stay. He even went twenty-one days without food and water. Most people knew him as Rev. Pryor or Gene Pryor, but the real man of God, they didn't have a clue. He was a man truly after God's own heart.

Staying Faithful through Challenges

We would spend as much time together as possible, and we kept our marriage alive even when we had it hard with the pressures of life being a pastor, father, and a mother. He had another family to take care of, and when you are a pastor, you have many families you are responsible for making sure you are leading them the way God said. Whatever God said, that is what Gene did. People don't realize when God calls a man or woman to preach (I did say call), God is the one in charge, not man. God had blessed us with our second daughter, Ruth Nicole, and God had plans we didn't see right then. God let Gene and I know he wasn't finished working miracles.

At the age of eleven years old, Nicole got sick with influenza, and one lung collapsed, and the other was damaged. She was out of school a year due to hospital stay. Satan was trying to stop God's plan, and that was not going to happen, but it didn't stop him from trying. We just kept praying and turning our plate down, whatever we had to do until God healed her, and he did. Oh, thank you Jesus, God, we love you.

Satan worked hard trying to put a stumbling block in the way, but Gene would go and pray. One day, he went out to pray for weeks or until God would give him an answer. While he was gone, I kept praying, "Lord, don't let anyone die while he is gone." He would leave, and some other preacher would preach while he was gone. One day, he came back, and I ran to him. He opened the door, and he was so frail he fell in my arms. I took him and nursed him back so that he would be able to go back to church.

We had God's favor in our lives because when we got saved, we sold out to God. He is everything to us. We had been at White Oak for a few years, and one day Gene said to God, "I want to see my angel," and God said to him, "It will hurt you," but he wanted to see him anyway.

If you obey God and do his will, he will answer your prayer. He said he would, and he can't lie.

God blessed us with three more children, Kimberly, Todd, and a beautiful baby girl name Shakita. Now we had four girls and three boys.

God answered our prayer, and we can't stop now, never. God is everything to us. We wouldn't have anything if it was not for God. Thank you, Lord, for saving us. We were on our way to a burning hell; that's why we are running for our lives ever since. We also must take some time out for our children. When things were good and when things were not so good, we knew that was part of life; our children were growing up. Their dad was trying to do some things to keep the boys off the street.

CHAPTER 9

Working through Tough Times

Count it all joy when ye fall into divers temptations;
knowing this, that the trying of your faith worketh
patience. But let patience have her perfect work, that
ye may be perfect and entire, wanting nothing.

—James 1:2-4

During the time we had to take care of our family, the church family, and also his sister family, and he worked a full-time job. I would get up early in the morning to fix breakfast from scratch so he would have a hot meal. It would be his favorite food he liked to eat, and I made sure Gene was always clean.

My washing machine stopped working, but I didn't let that stop me. I would fill up my bathtub with water and put in my clothes and cleaning powder. My children and I got in the tub and walked on the clothes to get them cleaned. Oh, the children and I had so much fun! They loved playing in the water. Oh yes, they were clean and hanging in the sun. I made my starch and ironed them for my family.

Sometimes for fun we would take the children to the airport just to see the planes come and go. When we could, we took them on trips.

Gene would work cutting grass away from home, and I would always surprise him with his favorite food, sweet potato pie, fried chicken. Lots of good times we laughed, we had so much fun, just our private picnics. Gene was so proud of his family.

I thank God for giving me my dream, the good, the bad, the pain, and the joy. All of this was in God's plan.

CHAPTER 10

Training to Be Men

Jesus said unto him, If thou canst believe, all
things are possible to him that believeth.

— Mark 9:23

ur oldest daughter, Betty, was nine months old when Gene
bought her a pony. Ever since then, he bought horses for
our boys when they got older; they bought and sold them.
They are men now. With their horses, oldest son, and two other
friends started a horse club, and it has grown from three boys
now and our other two sons have joined them. Also, the group
has grown to about eleven members now, our grandson sons are
riding also, they are buying selling and breeding horses and the
rest of our grandchildren. Gene and I are proud of them.

Their father was still riding with them for a few years. He would use this time when they were having trail rides, and he would witness to the people about God. Some of them got saved wherever we went. We brought up God's name, trying to leave some word about the Lord.

Also, with his sons and grandsons training them to ride, boys and girls, Gene loved spending time with his children. He also had a special horse he had got, and Gene called the horse Old Man. One day, he went to check on all the horses, and Old Man had gotten sick and couldn't get up. He was dying; it was late in the evening, and Gene got ready to leave. He knew that when he came back the next morning, he would have to bury the horse, but before he left, he looked at the horse and said a prayer then he said, oh man live. The next morning, he went back, and the first horse Gene saw standing at the gate was Old Man waiting on him. All things are possible with God for them that believes (Mark 9:23). Thank you, Lord!

CHAPTER 11

The Angel in the House – "Baby Named Corry"

And whatsoever ye shall ask in my name, that will
I do, that the Father may be glorified in the Son. If
ye shall ask any thing in my name, I will do it.

— John 14:13–14

Gene and I love the Lord, and we know we could ask God for anything in Jesus' name, and he would do it. Remember, I said a while ago Gene asked God to see his angel? The Lord had said, "It will hurt you if you do," but he wanted to see his angel anyway.

Our oldest daughter at the age of nineteen years old, the one I had so much trouble trying to get here, the doctor wanted to keep me in bed rest for nine months. He said, "You must because you are having problems bringing her to full term." The enemy didn't want her here; the devil tried to stop the plan of God. In Matthew 19:26, Jesus says with man this is impossible, but with God all things are possible.

Betty was the one at the age of nineteen years old, God had planned for her to carry her father's angel. The enemy was so angry she was so sick, in and out of the hospital the whole time, and the doctor was trying to keep her from having the baby too early. He was so small and was coming too soon when he was born; he weighed four pounds, and he had to stay in the hospital a month or two. We had no idea what was about to happen.

Our faith was being put to the test. We thought it would be just for a month that the baby would be in the hospital. We had experienced miracles, signs, and wonders, and also supernatural things. We had been through a lot of things and had seen a lot of things, but never anything like this. God said, "If ye abide in me, and my words abide in you, ye shall ask what ye will, and it shall be done unto you" (John 15:7). God says just live for me, and I will see you through it all; obey my word. But remember what Gene asked God for. When the baby Corry came, he was so sick he had bowel problems in his intestines, and it brought about many problems.

During his lifetime, he went to four different hospitals. Corry had fifty-six major operations; I believe we were in more pain than Corry from all that he went through. He never cried or complained about pain. He just didn't like being the center of attention. He didn't like that.

Corry had all kinds of problems one day. His lung started bleeding; after that, he could walk a little like a three-year-old pushing his walker on the floor, miracles!

Something else went wrong; the doctor came in, and Corry's heart strain had broken. He had to have another operation, this time on his heart. The doctor said they might lose him on the table. He wanted to know what to do, so Corry's mother, Gene, and I all agreed for the doctor to do what he needed to do; we knew God was in charge. The doctor said the heart strain was like a hair strain. He would have to go find it and put it back. If it took too much time, we might lose him on the table. We took it to God as always, and Betty knew she had our support and God's will would be done.

Gene and I never gave up on God and knew it would work out after a while. The doctor came back and said, "When I went in, the heart string was right there." All he had to do was just put it back together, thank God.

Romans 8:28 says, "And we know that all things work together for good to them that love God, to them who are called according to his purpose." God did it again. We had to trust in the Lord, but the devil never gave up. He fought hard. When he knows God has plans for you to carry out, when we come out of one, we go back into another. Times got harder. Our faith was tested many times. Sometimes at the hospital, we didn't have anywhere to stay. Betty slept on the floor or in her chair. Sometimes I was with her, and her sister slept on the floor and chairs. Maybe if she were lucky, she could stay at the McDonald house; you might get to stay one night a week. When you went out, you would have to carry your things with you and never leave your things behind. It stayed full almost all the time, so you had to be prepared to sleep on the floor or chair.

Corry didn't stay in the hospital for months, but for years we learned to take one day at a time. We never knew what tomorrow would bring. We only lived one day at a time. Corry's mother, Betty, had to grow up fast. She was very young, and God kept her. She stayed by Corry's side all his life, crying sometimes. We was afraid sometimes, yes, the whole family had to go through this, but it was all in God 's plan.

Corry got to a place and Betty was able to come home for five days and go back every week. She got married and had another son. Her mother-in-law kept her son, and she saw him on the weekend. Sometimes it was hard on their marriage; when you are young and have to always be ready to go and stay at the hospital. She and I and sometimes her sister, but her father, being a pastor of a church, we had our children at home, and we had another family. We were guardians of his sister's family plus the church family, and only God could get us through this.

After about six years, he was able to come home, but that was a different kind of heartache. We thought everything was getting better. We prayed and asked God to let Corry come home so the other children could get to see him, and they could love him. Corry came, but he was still in and out of the hospital. One day, he had to go back in for a while; he had edema. He had swollen up in his face. His legs and arms were so small when he went back this time, it shocked the people.

Corry was lying in bed, and the machine was going off like he had died. It looked like his heart had stopped beating, but Corry was laying there, sucking his fingers. His heart was not beating, but Corry was looking and talking to the doctors and nurses. No, this child was supposed to be dead, the machine said he was, but God was saying, "I am in charge." 1 Peter 3:12 says, "For the eyes of the Lord are over the righteous, and his ears are open unto their prayers."

The nurses came in to get his blood; they tried everywhere they could, and still blood wasn't coming out. They didn't understand, so Corry said, "Get it here in this finger." They tried the finger and feet both; he just said, "Get it here." There were many things that happened in our lives concerning him. Remember what I said a while back: It had gotten so things were happening.

You had to be in God to believe it—miracles, signs, and wonders were being seen in this child and around this child.

One day, the caseworker for the hospital came to Corry's room and asked if she could carry Corry down the hall to talk to him, and she would come back soon. Corry talked to her when she came back.

She asked me, "Mrs. Pryor, do you believe in reincarnation?"

I said, "No. Why?"

She said, "I talked to him, and what he said to me is he has been here before."

I didn't ask her what he said to her, but that was no surprise to us because of our own experience.

With him, Gene and I would lay in bed and talk to each other about Corry and wonder who he was, but at the time we wasn't thinking about what Gene had asked God for. Gene and I never talked very much about what Corry was doing and what the family had experienced. We call him Corry, but the Spirit of God was saying to us we gave him the name Corry, but he was not Corry.

He carried his grandfather Gene's T-shirt with him everywhere he went. He carried it to church, bed, hospital, riding around, or just sitting at home. He never wanted to depart from that T-shirt. Only when he went to sleep, I could wash it. He never wanted a new shirt; the shirt he had never departed from him. Corry never wanted it out of his sight. Gene and I knew God had sent Corry here, but we had to wait it out and just trust God for the answer. God was in charge. Oh Lord, what are you saying, miracles? We were seeing God move in this family.

CHAPTER 12

Supernatural

Let brotherly love continue. Be not forgetful
to entertain strangers: for thereby some
have entertained angels unawares.

—Hebrews 13:1-2

One day, his mother Betty, and Kim, our other daughter, and Corry were sitting in the den. Betty and Kim fell asleep for a minute. Corry was sitting in the other chair. They woke up and looked for him, and they couldn't find him. He never got down to run or played like other children; he was a serious type of child. They were worried and didn't know where he went, but before she could call for help to find him, something told her to sit down, and oh God, what is this?

A big light came down from the top of the house and lit in the chair, the light went out, and there Corry was sitting. Gene and I came in just as it was happening. Betty and Kim were trying to tell us, so I asked, "Corry did you leave?"

He said, "Yes ma'am."

I said, "Where did you go?" and just as fast as I asked him that in the same breath, I said, "Don't tell me," and many other signs took place. He laid hands, and God will heal. We were seeing these things happening with our natural eyes.

Remember Hebrews 13:1-2: "Let brotherly love continue. Be not forgetful to entertain strangers: for thereby some have entertained angels unawares."

So many other things happened. He was so small he wasn't able to do like other children, like go to school or play ball, but he liked to color and to take a pencil and color with it. He never ran out the side of the paper; he was at the age of four years old then. Corry and I would do things together or he would just help me to strain beans. He enjoyed this as his grandmother; Corry loved helping me.

Also, he loved church. He would sing with the children, and he would pray and talk to the older people. We have had some adults that he talked to about their problems. When he talked to adults about some things, we never asked him what they said. He wouldn't talk about it anyway.

One day, Corry was sitting on the couch. He looked down the hall and said, "Papa, if I go somewhere, will God be there?"

Gene looked, and Corry was smiling, so Gene looked to see what Corry saw, and it was like a kingdom so bright all he could say, was, "This boy is leaving me," and when he said papa so loud, it was different. I knew he was leaving. "Oh God, he is about to leave us."

Then Gene came out of the house where I was, and I said, "Gene, the next time Corry goes to the hospital, I am going to ask God to take him home with him." I didn't know what he had just said to his grandfather.

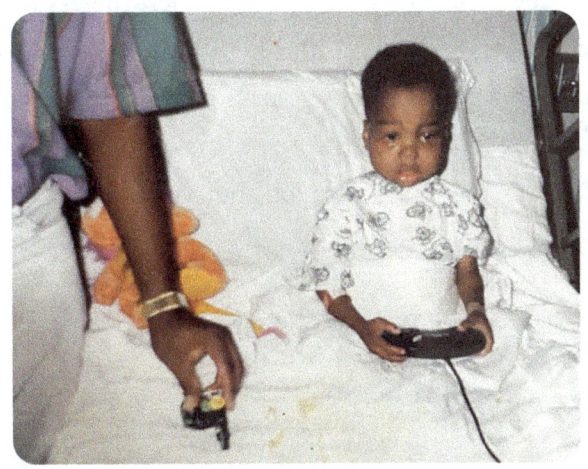

Corry had time to spend with his three brothers. They loved each other. When we would go to church and any place, people would give him money. He would stop at our little table, and he would take out all his money and say to his mother, "You take this money and buy milk and this and buy Pampers, and this is yours, and this is mine." Corry thought of them before himself.

After I said that to Gene, Betty came to pick up the boys, but I had to carry out Corry when I picked him up. He hugged me so tight as he went out the door. I said, "Oh baby, you are hugging Grandma so tight." I didn't know it was my last time to get a big hug from him. Always remember to love one another. You never know when is your last time seeing each other or your loved one.

The next morning, Betty called early. She said, "Mama, Daddy, come quick, it's Corry."

His father, Trini, was always by his side when we got there. All emergency personnel were there. Corry called for Papa Gene, and he said, "I am here."

The rescue people took Corry, and he left the T-shirt behind. Corry kept that T-shirt with him for about five or six years and never left it, but now at the age of nine years old, Corry's task was over, Gene said, then the Spirit spoke to him and said, "I told you it was going to hurt you, but you wanted to see your angel anyway."

Corry Was the Angel in the House

So many people have been blessed by God and Corry to this world. He was small and stature, but so great. God, I am so thankful for what God is done in our family. Thank God for my three boys and four girls with fifteen grandchildren and eight great grandchildren, and all twenty-three.

You see, God will give you what you asked if you just trust him. Love God with all your heart and obey his Word and pray, and he will guide you. The Lord is saying every day we can still trust him in our lives. We have been up and down but never seen the righteous forsaken nor his seeds begging for bread.

As I said, I have been blessed. Our daughter Nicole, the one who was so sick at the age of eleven years old, God called her to preach at the age fourteen, but she had to wait on God. We thought it would be hard for her to sing again with one lung, but God fixed that. Let me know. I am still here. You just think back over life. God gave me just about everything I have asked for and more.

God said if we ask anything according to his will he hears us (1 John 5:14). My desire is to always please God. Sometimes I feel like I have failed, and I've come short, but I will go to my secret closet to pray to make sure everything is all right with me. When I think about him, I know he was there all the time. I always check my life out. God wants us to always stay at the foot of the Cross when we feel weak. God wants us to be strong through it all. I have learned to trust him. Life gets tough sometimes, but we will overcome someday. Never give up on God—he won't give up on you.

Gene and I were still working for God's kingdom. God was still blessing at the Oak. We had been at White Oak Springs now for about forty-five years. Gene asked God why people were not getting healed at the church. God said to him, and Gene said to the church, when he prays for someone to get healed, the Spirit said call their name. There was a man at the point of death, and Gene said we got to call his name. He was not able to get out of his bed.

Rev. Pryor said, "Church, we must call his name. God will heal him," and we did. Gene said, "We will call it together," and the man got up, and God healed him. The Lord gave him a new liver. The doctor said they didn't know what happened, but we know he has a new liver. The man got up and painted his house.

After that, many names were called, and God healed many. Remember Jesus brought Lazarus back from the dead. We thank

God for what he has done in our lives; we have seen people come to Christ, many have gotten saved and grown stronger in the Lord, and Gene and I were getting a little older, in our seventies. At the returning age, he was not able to walk very well but still preaching.

A Man After God's Own Heart

We had a lot of things yet to do. He turned his plate down again and went to talk to God. He told the church, "I am trying to fix this."

He said to the church, "People are coming, and they are coming in hurry. You all better get ready." Then he said, "Make sure your name is written in the Lamb's Book of Life. If it's not, you can't get in. It's like this: If you go to a hotel to check in, if your name is not on the book, you can't get in, so make sure. If not, you better get it in the book of life." Then Reverend said, "My name is there!" He gave a big smile and shouted out.

Then he asked another question: "And who would give his life for me?" Then he said, "God said in John 15:13-14, 'Greater love hath no man than this, that a man lay down his life for his friends.' Jesus said ye are my friend if ye do whatsoever, I command you." Gene loved God with all his heart. He said, "To go to heaven, you must believe you are going."

So Gene asked me that evening, "Ruth, are you going to heaven?"

I said, "Yes, Gene, you know I am going to heaven."

He was praying all the time. Gene never made a move without God. When he was telling us what he was asking God for, there was so much more to be done. Gene always taught that you can't leave until your work is done, but it is still a lot more to be done at the church and he knew it, so he said to me, "Ruth, I am trying to fix this."

He was talking to God about him coming home to heaven. Gene's work was about to be over, and he was trying to prepare us and was waiting on God's answer, but he was not going to quit on us. Gene knew, but he was willing to lay down his life. He was still reaching out for souls to be saved. Rev. Bennie Gene Pryor wasn't a quitter. His time had come.

I was lying down, and he was still up looking at TV about 10:00 or 11:00 p.m. that night, March 27, 2020. I believe God sent Gene's angel Corry, and Gene came to the bedroom and said, "Ruth give me something." He had chest pain, he wouldn't go to the hospital, and I gave him something for the pain, hoping it would ease up. We were sitting there, and Gene and I were alone like we started, just the two of us.

He looked at me and said, "Ruth, am I sweating?"

I said, "No, not that I can tell."

Then he said, "Ruth, this is it." He took a long breath, and he was gone.

It seemed that my life stopped. I had lost my best friend, the love of my life, my partner. I just wanted to be held in his arms one last time. We met at an early age, and now we were old. We were married for fifty-five years. I met Gene at the age of nineteen, and he left me at the age of seventy-eight years old. He was the man I asked God for, the man of my dreams, the place I wanted to go he took me there, the husband, the father, God, our children and grandchildren, Gene loved dearly. I will always remember his special song to me, My Girl, he could only sing to me, and my heart would skip a beat.

CHAPTER 13

It Hurts

The Lord is nigh unto them that are of a broken
heart; and saveth such as be of a contrite spirit.

—Psalm 34:18

Now I must go on. The night he died, I went to my prayer room. I was so hurt, but I didn't know why. I said to the Lord, "Give me some of Gene's boldness." All my life, I was very shy to stand in front of people. Now I was in my prayer room, and when I came out, I had it. God granted it so fast.

We found out Gene was already working on the plan. God was giving him instruction. Many times he would tell me things. I wasn't catching it then, but now I know he told us before that day. You will know there had been a prophet amongst you. Our daughter Nicole had been preaching for a long time. Her dad gave her his pastor's manual and said to study it from front to back.

He was already making plans to leave to go home to be with the Lord after he died.

I was trying to make a decision on some things, and I said, "Lord, what shall I do?" The spirit spoke and gave me the answer, then God has never forsaken nor has he left me alone. Now that my husband is in heaven, I am eighty-two years old, and I'm trying to get my time in. Also, time is short, and I have many jobs to do. I am busy in church now working.

One Sunday morning, I was on my way to church, and I said, "Oh God, I need the Holy Ghost in order to do my job right," but I said, "I am willing to wait." I was about seven miles from the church, and when I got there, Pastor Nicole called me over.

She said, "Mother, come up here." She said, "The Lord said for me to lay hands on you," and she did, and I received the Holy Ghost. God is a right-now God. At the Oak, God is really moving. People are coming. They are being blessed. The Spirit is in the church. The Word is being taught and preached, and the blessings are flowing, all kinds. God is blessing with first spiritual blessings. This job, money being found, people getting healed.

Two years ago, I dreamed of a blue Cadillac. The pastor told us that the Spirit of God said, "This year will be one of our blessed years," and to tell the people to get your houses, jobs, cars, and money—some will be retiring early from supernatural blessings.

At the time she spoke it, she prayed for everyone and people were saying what they wanted. My daughter Pastor Nicole was talking, and I said to her, "I thought about a car," but I didn't say anything.

She said, "Mom, why not? You can have it if you just say it."

And I said, "I want a car," I said. "I want a special car." My favorite car is a Cadillac, so I said, "Lord, a Cadillac is what I want." So I went the next day, but it was a holiday, so we went the following day before the evening, everything was in the making, so the next day, I had my car. Oh yes, it was my dream car—the light blue Cadillac that I dreamed of two years earlier. God is pouring out blessings, and most of all, he is using our Pastor Nicole and the church, it is on fire for God.

That is what is all about God's work is going for. We know Reverend Bennie Gene Pryor prayed for the church, and that is one of the things he talked to God about before he left us, and his seed is our pastor. She is just like him; they have the same Spirit. She loves God. Reverend Gene Pryor is not with us in the flesh, but he is still with us in spirit.

I wanted to write this book to let you all know that God is real. He is taking care of me as always; my husband is gone now, my soulmate. The pain in my heart, it seems like it just doesn't want to go away. You don't know the hurt, the tears I hide behind a smile on my face, the sorrow hoping for a better tomorrow. I know God hears my cry.

Just the other night, I was having trouble, a spiritual attack on my mind. I was praying. It just seemed like I couldn't get through. I got up out of my bed. I was calling God. I sat up on the side of my bed, but I still couldn't get a breakthrough. I got up in my chair, still asking him to send my angel. I was troubled.

I got back in bed. I was still calling God; this attack had never happened before. I laid on my right side, and then as I was still praying before my face, I saw an angel with the long white rope. He reached his hands out under me and picked me up and rocked me in his arms. I did not see his hand, and I didn't see his face, but he was so tall. In his arms, I was so small. I can't remember when he put me down, but then I was in a dream. I was telling people what just happened to me, and after that my problems were gone.

CHAPTER 14

God Heard My Cry

But seek ye first the kingdom of God,
and his righteousness; and all these
things shall be added unto you.

—Matthew 6:33

All my life God has been with me, through the ups and downs. I have learned to keep God first. God must be first, not last, in your life. Try and read your Bible. If you fall, get up, repent, and God will forgive. Ask me how I know—I have made many mistakes. I cried out to God, and he took me back, but after I kept trying, I got strong enough to stand.

Praise God every day. Take one day at a time, and keep looking up! Jesus could come anytime now. He said watch and pray.

God said be ready. I want to write about my life. Maybe it will help someone. Now I have finished it and hope it will help you to keep the faith, no matter what comes your way.

My husband's wish was that I write a book about us, so I set out to try my best. It seemed like everything came back to me as if it was yesterday. I thank God. He has never left me. I was looking back on my life and was trying so hard, but I had to go back and remember God's Word in Mark 9:23. Jesus said if you can believe, all things are possible to him who believes.

John 3:16 says that for God so loved the world that he gave his only begotten son, that whoever believes in him should not perish, but have everlasting life. Thank you, Jesus. I try every day to stay in the Word and to talk to God always. Jesus said in Matthew 4:4, "It is written, man shall not live by bread alone, but by every word that proceedeth out of the mouth of God."

I live every day to be a better person that God can count on. Now I have written this book in the memory of my husband, Reverend Bennie Gene Pryor, born January 1, 1942, death March 27, 2020. Gene was seventy-eight, and I am now eighty-two, and this is our story, God bless.

Gene and I tried to bring our children up like the Bible said, teaching and praying with them. We made a lot of mistakes as young parents. But we kept praying that God would help us; it was not easy with Gene pastoring, and we carried our children to church, to revivals, church trips out of town, and we took time for them to let them know we loved them.

Now they are older and have taken their own paths, but they are still around and now they are loving us back trying to take care of us. They had a lot of fun with us when the children and grandchildren came over. It was so much fun just being with our children. Gene would laugh so hard until he cried. Now he is no longer here in the flesh. He is with us in spirit.

Our children now take care of me very well. Their dad said, "Take care of her, give her what she wants," and my children take care of me very well. My God is still with me. When God caught my husband, God never left me at any time I needed him. He will always show up, somehow, some way. Now that my husband is no longer here, all my time I can spend talking and praying to God. I have told you about the supernatural things early in the book.

Prayer

Dear God,

Thank you for giving me the wisdom and the knowledge to write this book. It has been a very long time coming, but, Lord, you have been there for me. Thank you for bringing me through my troubles. You never left me when I was in tears. You wiped them away when my burdens got so hard to bear. You took my burden away.

I pray that this book will help someone to find a way to you, Lord, this is my prayer, and I hope someone gets saved. I was lost, but you saved me, thank you, God. By reading my book someone may see how you brought me through, and Lord, you will bring them through also. Whatever state they are in, I pray that they give it to you. They can call you night or day. God, you love us and always are ready to answer our call, in Jesus' name I pray, Amen.

Thank you, Jesus, for making my dream come true.

Ruth Pryor

About the Author

Ruth Allen Pryor is a homemaker and former first lady, with a dream of sharing her love story of her husband and her love of Christ. She comes with a plethora of experience with raising children in a God-fearing environment, while supporting her husband as he traveled the world reclaiming lives to Christ. She is the mother of seven children and one godson. She has fifteen grandchildren and seven great-grandchildren.

Inspired by a lifelong love of taking care of her family, supporting her husband, and loving God, Ruth was compelled to share her life of triumph, love, and faith. Ruth has devoted her life of eighty-two years to empowering others, leading a life full of love, and serving God with everything in her being. She has forty-three years of experience with being a first lady of the former White Oak Springs Baptist Church, where her husband was the pastor until his untimely passing in 2020.

Being led by the Holy Spirit, Ruth has embarked on the journey to tell her love story of how she met her husband and how she has learned to trust God while building her most holy faith.

Ruth is currently serving at White Oak Springs International Church Ministries as the mother of the church. She is under the leadership of her daughter, who resided as pastor after the passing of her husband, Pastor Bennie G. Pryor. Ruth continues to lead the church kitchen committee, intercessory team, pastor's aid and visionary of the ministry.

www.ingramcontent.com/pod-product-compliance
Lightning Source LLC
Chambersburg PA
CBHW060954120626
46557CB00003B/1157

* 9 7 8 1 9 6 1 0 6 5 1 9 2 *